ILLUSIONS OF

CHOICE

The Hidden Hand of

Astrology behind US

Presidential Elections

MK Weale

Published by Epic Truth

Illusions of Choice

The Hidden Hand of Astrology behind US Presidential Elections

Website:

www.forepictruth.com

Contact Us:

forepictruth@gmail.com

ISBN: 978-0-9989919-0-0
LCCN: 2017941982

1st Edition - June 2017

Published by Epic Truth
Show Low, AZ

Dedication

This book is dedicated to my daughter Anna,

My loving Aries Ram,

Fire of my Life,

Forever inseparable among the Stars

Table of Contents

Introduction

Have you ever wondered why it seems like US presidential election follows a set pattern or cycle every eight years? Democrats and Republicans seem to alternate terms like the changing of the guard. Corporations all seem to benefit no matter what industry they are in; defense, health, banking, food, etc. It all just functions as too perfect of a system. It's almost as if there exists a hidden force. A hidden hand that controls who and what party becomes elected at a specific time in history. Despite all the campaign rhetoric, drama, attacks, scandals, trench ads, policy positions, and surrogates, in the end, the outcome fits a predictable pattern.

Why is this so repeatable and predictable?

Even the timing of the election campaign cycle has a very distinct timing pattern from the start of the primary campaigns, conventions, election, through the inauguration.

Is this just random planning, voting trends, or political convenience? Or is there something else at play?

Things are more scientific in the age of reason now, but the founders of the United States in the era of 1776 had more understanding and balanced the use of both scientific and metaphysical principles. For example, the layout and architecture of Washington D.C. has been researched extensively and found to be designed based on astronomical and metaphysical principles. Many books, documentaries, and movies have explored this in detail.

What most people are not aware of is that the US presidential election process is based on astronomical and metaphysical principles just like the layout of the nation's capital. Once metaphysics is factored in, the timing and energetic impulse of events, political parties, candidates, and election outcomes becomes amazingly more clear, purposeful, and predictable.

Once you read this book you will never look at the US presidential election in the same way again.

This book details the hidden metaphysical principles involved in the US presidential election process using a combination of astrology, timing, cycles, candidate data, and history. You do not need to be an astrologer to read and understand this book, it is written for a general audience. Some people like charts and graphs, some like information presented and explained in narrative form. I have strived to provide both in this book.

My background is in engineering and business analytics. I use this background to define data, cycles, and patterns, as objectively and analytically as I can. I treat astrology as I would any other natural science. The data is either there to support a theory or conclusion or not. I look at facts, data, and trends, not what I expect, believe, or hope something to be.

The astrological zodiac system used in this book is the sidereal system. The sidereal system is the most ancient astrological system dating back to the cradle of civilization in ancient Babylon and was also used by Mayan, ancient Egyptian and Greece astrologers, as well as the Vedic astrologers of today. Since the sidereal system was the original zodiac system taught to humans in Babylon; that is the system used in this book. The sidereal system also closely agrees with the placement of constellations, stars, and planets scientist and astronomers have identified and use today they call the IAU or International Astronomical Union zodiac (see Appendix I). The IAU zodiac does have 13 signs, whereas the sidereal zodiac has 12 signs. The ancients considered the 13th sign, Ophiuchus, to be the hidden sign, and therefore absorbed it into the signs of Scorpio and Sagittarius as part of the 12 sign constellation system most people are familiar with today. The hidden sign was only used by the most secret and powerful inner circles.

Humankind was first taught astrology when the space beings (also referred to as the Watchers or Angels), came to Earth and participated in Earth history that eventually led to the Earth humans we are today. It is documented in detail in an ancient Jewish religious text called the Book of Enoch (see Appendix II). In the Ethiopian version, dated to the 3rd century B.C., 1 Enoch (1-36), describes that the Watcher Baraqel (also spelled Baraqijal, Baraqiel) taught humans astrology.[1] The Book of Enoch is not included in the Judeo-Christian Bible, but is considered inspired by the Ethiopian Orthodox Church. There are references to Enoch in both the Old and New Testament of the Bible. [2]

Chapter 1
Timing is Everything

Timing is everything when it comes to most things in life. If you think about it, when you started grade school, high school, or college, became an adult, celebrated holidays, started working, purchased a house or car, or signed an important contract; these major events and transitions happened at set times and ages in your life. An astrologer would say that creation chose a specific time and place for you to be born that created your birth chart so you could be a certain person, of a particular personality, and experience specific energies in this life as the next step in your evolutionary journey as a universal being.

If we approach the US presidential election in the same way it also has a set timing mechanism to its cycle. The founders of America were well versed in metaphysics and used universal principles to determine the timing for the best potential outcomes based on constellational and planetary influences. The founders who most influenced the definition of the election cycle were Benjamin Franklin who was famous for his Almanacs used for planting crops which relied on astrological influences such as the moon phases, George Washington who was a Freemason, and Thomas Jefferson who was familiar with philosophy and esoteric principles and understood the significance of the astrological cycles such as the solstices and equinoxes, as well as constellation and planetary influences.

The US Constitution was created by the founders in 1787. The term of the president was defined in Article II, Section I, it states:

"The executive power shall be vested in a President of the United States of America. He shall hold his office during the term of four years ...." [3]

The term of four years likely was chosen due to the number four's ancient esoteric meaning among philosophical and secret orders, such as Freemasonry. The number four in philosophy and Kabbalah (mystical Judaism), represents material manifestation (such as the four cardinal directions of the Earth; east, west, north, south), perfection, and the name of God. In antiquity the name of God was always spelled with four letters. For example, in the Jewish tradition it was spelled YHWH. [4]

Synthesizing the meaning of the number four and applying it to the term of the US Presidency it is the set or perfect time of the material manifestation of God's appointed representative upon the US.

Another esoteric principal applied to the US presidential election cycle is the date of the current Election Day. In 1845 it was specified as the first Tuesday after the first Monday in November by Congress (which falls sometime between November 2nd and 8th) to address the problem of voter fraud in presidential elections, which went into effect in 1848. Astrologically this is significant because it always places the date of the Election in the sidereal sign of Libra, ruled by Venus. The significance of this sign and ruler as a part of an astrological theme applied to the entire election cycle will be examined in detail in this book.

James K. Polk was President of the US from 1845-1849, which was during the time period of the setting of the Election Day Congressional rule. He was a confirmed Freemason and would have been familiar with the influences of the planets and constellations, especially Venus. In fact, many of the US Presidents in this timeframe were Free Masons as shown in Table 1.

Free Mason President	Term of Office
James Monroe	1817- 1825
Andrew Jackson	1829- 1837
James K. Polk	1845- 1849
James Buchanan	1857- 1861
Andrew Jackson	1865- 1869

Table 1   **Free Mason Presidents in Mid 1800's** [5]

There were also many other politicians who were Freemasons in the Congress in Washington, D.C. This would suggest a strong Masonic esoteric influence in legislation existed in this time period, including any legislation affecting the major milestone dates of the US Presidential Election process.

Let's look at the major steps in the election process and their astrologically significance for 2016 election cycle per Table 2.

Astrological Sign/Planetary Ruler/Symbol	Milestone Event	Date
Capricorn/Saturn /Goat	Primaries Begin	Feb 1 (Iowa primary is first)
Taurus/Venus /Bull	Primaries End	June 14
Cancer/Moon/ Crab	Republican Convention Democratic Convention	July 18-21 July 25-28
Libra/Venus Scales	Election Day	Nov 8
Capricorn/Saturn /Goat	Inauguration	Jan 20*

* By law the new President must be sworn in by January 20th. Sometimes the public ceremony is later.

Table 2   US Presidential Election Cycle 2016

The first thing of note is that there are three planets that control and manage election event timing; Saturn, Venus, and the Moon. The primaries start in the sign of Capricorn represented by its symbol of the steady footed Goat which is ruled by Saturn. Capricorn is a sign that is associated with big business, money, and management. It knows how to manage complex, large enterprises such as corporations and government that involve budgeting and spending large amounts of money. Saturn in astrology controls time, structure, and authority. So it is fitting that the US presidential election cycle started in the sign of Capricorn ruled by Saturn.

Taurus, whose symbol is the Bull, controls ownership and possessions. Venus rules partnerships and rewards. When the primaries ended, the partnership with the winning party candidate was determined and ownership accepted.

The conventions were held in Cancer the Crab the sign of emotions, such as feelings and devotion. Cancer is ruled by the Moon which is one of the two luminary planets in the solar system. The luminaries are associated with light and power. The Moon illumines which party candidate will now lead. The conventions are held in Cancer to rally the support for the party and emotionally connect the support of the candidate with the voters. At the culmination of the convention the candidate accepts the nomination of the party and their confirmation as the party candidate to represent them in the general election.

On Election Day, the partnership of the President elect is sealed with the voters through Venus in Libra represented by the symbol of the Scales; as the voters weigh the candidates on Libra's scale of justice and act as judge and juror of the election.

The inauguration happens in Capricorn the Goat of the next year as Saturn finalizes the process at the set time defined by law. The new President is installed by Saturn and is now given the authority to govern.

Look at how nicely the influence of the astrological signs, planets, and rulers just described fit with the US presidential election cycle major milestone events. It makes logical sense as to why these event milestones happen when they do. Do you think this is just a random correlation or set at times of convenience? Or do you think there is purpose behind why these election cycle events happen when they do; the hidden force alluded to in the Introduction of this book behind the timing of events?

Venus especially plays a key role in determining party candidates and who the election winner is. Venus rules both the sign of Taurus (the time period when primaries end and party candidates are chosen) and Libra (the time period when the election occurs and the president is elected) as Table 2 shows. As this book progresses it will continue to build on the pivotal role Venus plays in who is elected President.

From an astrological viewpoint, there is just too much correlation throughout the election process for it to all be just chance occurrences. It's not surprising because many of the founders in pivotal roles in the early design of the election process were educated in esoteric principles and understood the astrological influences at work in the Universe. They applied this knowledge to the election process to assure the best outcome for the country. They knew the value of timing significant events to be harmonious with the natural cycles of the Universe and planet Earth. The principles of astrology have continued to be applied to changes in the US Presidential election process into modern times as demonstrated when term limits were imposed. In the next Chapter we will explore this in detail.

Chapter 2
The Morning Star

Franklin Roosevelt was elected to four terms as President of the United States in the 1930's and 1940's, and then died in office during his fourth term at a very critical time during World War II, which necessitated that the Vice President Harry Truman take over as President.

After the war, the American people pressed Congress to impose a limit on the number of terms a President could serve. They felt Roosevelt had been in power for too long and although he was considered a great President of the people, he had become very ill during his last term in office and the Presidency had become very taxing on him during a critical time of war. If he had not been able to serve for four terms, then his death in office during WW II could have been avoided.

In 1947 the 22nd Amendment to the US Constitution was presented to Congress and was subsequently ratified by the required number of States and became law on February 27, 1951. It reads as follows:[6]

Section 1. No person shall be elected to the office of the President more than twice, and no person who has held the office of President, or acted as President, for more than two years of a term to which some other person was elected President shall be elected to the office of the President more than once. But this article shall not apply to any person holding the office of President when this article was proposed by the Congress, and shall not prevent any person who may be holding the office of President, or acting as President, during the term within which this article becomes operative from holding the office of President or acting as President during the remainder of such term.

Section 2. This article shall be inoperative unless it shall have been ratified as an amendment to the Constitution by the legislatures of three-fourths of the several states within seven years from the date of its submission to the states by the Congress.

This amendment to the US Constitution now limits the Presidency to a maximum of two terms of 4 years each (8 years total) for President's serving from February 27, 1951 and on. During the Presidential election cycle in 1952 this new constitutional amendment was in effect for the first time.

Astrologically this term limit of eight years is very significant. This is also the synodic cycle of Venus and the Earth. The synodic cycle of Venus and Earth is the time Venus takes to be seen again from the Earth in the same position with respect to the Sun. It is about 584 days long (see Appendix III). This means that **Venus repeats its cyclical energy pattern every eight years. On Election Day every eight years it does something VERY, VERY special astrologically, the Planet Venus goes "Out of**

Bounds". This has been the case in Presidential elections since 1952!

Let's take a look now at the Presidential election results between 1952 and the most recent cycle of 2016 in eight year increments.

Year	President Elect	Party
1952	Eisenhower	Republican
1960	Kennedy	Democrat
1968	Nixon	Republican
1976	Carter	Democrat
1984	Reagan	Republican
1992	Clinton	Democrat
2000	G.W. Bush	Republican
2008	Obama	Democrat
2016	Trump	Republican

Table 3 - Eight Year Term Cycles from 1952

What do you notice repeating every eight years?

The party in power alternates every 8 years. Even when something unexpected happens during a Presidency such as the assassination of Kennedy, resignation of Nixon, or Carter not being elected to a second term; at the 8 year Venus synodic cycle interval where an "Out of Bound" occurs, the Party changes. This has happened consistently 9 times in a row since 1952.

The US Electoral process is designed to support a 2 Party system. Even when there are other Parties in the election cycle, such as Independent, Green, Libertarian, etc.; as the election approaches voters align with one of the two major parties most likely to win, Republican or Democrat. It takes 270 Electoral votes to win, so if 3 parties were split evenly in the vote it would create a big problem, no one would be able to achieve the 270 electoral votes, and this would cause Congress to choose the next President.

The probability that the ultimate victor would not represent any kind of majority of the choice of the people is not what the citizens want, so there is a natural shift towards a candidate for each of the two major Parties the closer the election approaches. That's not to say that one day a new

Party may take the place of one of the existing two major parties, but it would still narrow down to be a 2 way race by Election Day. Let's say hypothetically in 2016 that Bernie Sanders would have chosen to continue running after Hillary Clinton became the Democratic convention Party nominee as an Independent. Either the Democratic Party or Independent candidate would have had to gain the upper hand, or they would have to consolidate energies at some point in order to present a viable candidate against the Republicans that was capable of amassing 270 electoral votes. In 2016 they consolidated their energy under the Democratic Party by the time the Democratic Convention occurred.

Every 8 years during the Venus "Out of Bounds" a new Party is elected causing the priorities of government to change. Generally speaking, Democrats are more focused on global and social issues, and Republicans are more focused on fiscal and privatization issues. Below is an example of how the Parties differ on their initiatives:

Democratic Initiatives	Republican Initiatives
Universal Healthcare	Private Healthcare
Climate Change Regulation	Energy Development Deregulation
Gun Control	Gun Rights
Entitlements	Jobs
Global Trade Treaties	Free Trade Treaties
Pro Choice	Pro Life
Federal Public Education	State Public Education
Open Borders	Immigration Control
Banking/Investment Regulations	Banking/Investment Deregulation
Military Reduction	Military Investment

Table 4   Democratic vs. Republican Initiatives

The two parties are really polar opposites in their focus as to how to serve the country. What is really interesting is that the voters choose this shift between what appears to be polar opposites every 8 years, or do they?

Maybe Venus is the real vehicle of change? Do the citizens align with the energy of Venus during these "Out of Bounds" extremes every eight years without even being consciously aware of it?

The initiatives of the two major parties have been consistent for decades, so why would voters choose the exact opposite initiatives every 8 years? Some say factors such as demographic changes have a lot to do with it. This may be a factor to some extent. But there is more to it.

In 2016 Blacks and Hispanics were predicted to vote overwhelmingly for the Democrats, they didn't. Women were supposed to vote overwhelmingly for the Democratic first women candidate, they didn't. This is less about demographics and more about an overarching energy change. Venus "Out of Bounds" is an astrological condition that causes extreme change, and that is exactly what we are seeing every 8 years.

Did the powers behind the 22nd Amendment understand this power of Venus when they proposed the two term limit? You have to admit it maintains a balance of power in virtually every area of government and works every facet of government by going back and forth between parties every 8 years. Is Venus the ultimate check and balance agent of the US government built into our election process?

Venus is one of the brightest astronomical bodies in the Earth sky. We call it a planet, but in ancient times it was called a star. The ancients could measure the movement of Venus and were very aware of its cycles. They called it the "Morning Star" because it was the first star visible on the horizon when the Sun rose in the east.

Those familiar with metaphysics have known about the special astrological properties of Venus since ancient times. This knowledge has been passed down in philosophical groups, circles, guilds, lodges, etc. since the Watchers taught astrology and astronomy to humans. The elite or ruling class were taught astrological principles and used them as part of their decision making process. This is still true today and includes a significant number of politicians.

Albert Pike Masonic Sovereign Grand Commander of the Scottish Rite from 1859 until his death in 1891, in his book "Morals and Dogma" wrote this about Venus (referred to as Lucifer and Light):

"Lucifer, the Son of the Morning! Is it *he* who bears the *Light*, and with its splendors intolerable blinds feeble, sensual, or selfish Souls? Doubt it not!"[7]

Venus the Morning Star bears a very strong astrological influence or energy upon the Earth; we become wise when we come to understand its influences and embrace it.

The 22nd amendment to the constitution was initially proposed to Congress by Thomas E. Dewey, the 47th Governor of New York. He had lost two presidential elections, the first to Franklin D. Roosevelt in 1944 and the second to Harry S, Truman in 1948. After Roosevelt passed in office during his fourth term, Dewey proposed to Congress that there be a two term limit on the US President. Thomas Dewey was a well- known Freemason. He could have known as a Freemason, about the importance of Venus as the Morning Star and its metaphysical properties as is taught in many philosophical schools of thought. I believe it is very possible that there was a conscious effort to align the two term limit with the energies of Venus.

Do you think this was taken into consideration when they recommended a two term consecutive limit? In fact, the theory presented in this book is based on the premise that the entire election process has been designed to correspond to certain astrological energies by the ruling class familiar with esoteric concepts and their application.

Let's review, so far we have:

- the four year office of the President and election cycle is defined in the Constitution with the major designers such as George Washington, Benjamin Franklin, Thomas Jefferson, James Monroe, James Madison, Patrick Henry and many others who were Freemasons or closely associated with esoteric philosophy. The term of four years has a basis in sacred numerology.

- major events in the election cycle from the beginning of the primaries through the inauguration happen at predefined significant times in the astrological signs as shown in Table 2.

- the primaries end determining which of the major party candidates are chosen by getting the most primary votes determined in June during the sidereal sign of Taurus, a sign ruled by Venus

- The election occurs in early November, when the President elect is determined during the sidereal sign of Libra, a sign ruled by Venus

- Every eight years the party that won has changed since 1952 as shown in Table 3

- The major 2 parties, Democrats and Republicans, have generally polar opposite political positions as shown in Table 4

- The 22nd Amendment to the Constitution to limit the Presidency to two terms of eight years, was advocated By Thomas F. Dewey, a prominent Freemason.

- Venus and Earth have an eight year synodic cycle. This means Venus returns to the same place every eight years in regards to its alignment to Earth during the election cycle.

Every key aspect of the election process so far pivots off of Venus.

Chapter 3
Out of Bounds

We have seen that Venus plays a pivotal role in the election process every eight years. Why Venus? Why not one of the other planets in our solar system?

Jupiter is especially considered a beneficial planet, if not the most beneficial planet, to be activated in an astrology chart. Clients are always thrilled to have a Jupiter return coming up. That is a time when the client is considered favored by astrologers.

Why limit the Presidency to two terms of eight years? They could have chosen one term of four years or three terms of twelve years? Four years would make Presidents work quickly to make change. They would have to come into office with a very detailed plan and strategy of how to work with and get approval from Congress. Twelve years would allow more time to achieve compromises and get consensus with Congress on complex issues.

We discussed in Chapter 2 that Venus returns to the same out of bounds position every eight years on Election Day. The reason this occurs is because of the Venus-Earth synodic cycle. The word synod means "meeting". So it just means that The Earth and Venus meet, or an astrologer would say they align and have a conjunction in a particular astrological sign. The Venus-Earth synodic cycle is 1.6 years (584 days). Five of these cycles occur in an eight year period. **Every five synodic cycles the Earth and Venus have their conjunction on Election Day in the same sign of Libra.** This is one reason why the pentagram is so important in metaphysics, because Venus conjuncts with the Earth five times in eight years to form a five pointed conjunction star pattern. No other planet in the solar system has a synodic cycle with Earth that causes this pattern or occurs every eight years.

In Table 5 are the Earth synodic cycles for the other planets in our solar system:

Earth-Mercury	116 days
Earth-Mars	780 days (1.88 years)
Earth-Jupiter	399 days (approx. 13 months)
Earth-Saturn	378 days
Earth-Uranus	370 days
Earth-Neptune	367 days
Earth- Pluto	367 days

Table 5   **Earth Synodic Cycles** [8]

You can see that no other planet paired with the Earth can repeat its synodic cycle any number of times and end up at the same point in its synodic cycle on Election Day, whether you look at 4, 8, or 12 year increments of the Presidential terms.

In Physics they consider the solar system to be made up of waves and particles. Think of the Earth and Venus as really big particles and their movement pattern through the solar system as two waves of distinct frequency or vibration. The waves interact with each other to determine the harmonic or harmony with each other. It's like 2 people who want to get married need to be "on the same frequency" with each other. In other words, they need to be harmonious with each other. In the same way, some chords (combinations of different notes) in music are more harmonious than others. **The Earth-Venus harmonic (synodic cycle) is considered to be the most harmonious in the solar system.** Harmonics and combinations of frequencies of planets with the Earth are what the famous scientist, astrologer, and esoteric philosopher Johannes Keplar wrote about in 1619 in his famous work "Harmonices Mundi". Students of esoteric studies are very familiar with the concept of the Music of the Spheres through the works of Keplar as well as others such as Pythagoras. Its principles and use are also present in sacred geometry, numerology, and meditation. Freemasons would be very familiar with it.

The other factor we haven't looked at yet is the Out of Bounds condition. **An Out of Bounds condition means that a planet is orbiting beyond a declination (latitude) of 23.5 degrees outside the Tropic of Cancer or**

Capricorn. In astrology latitude is also referred to as declination. This is shown in Figure 1.

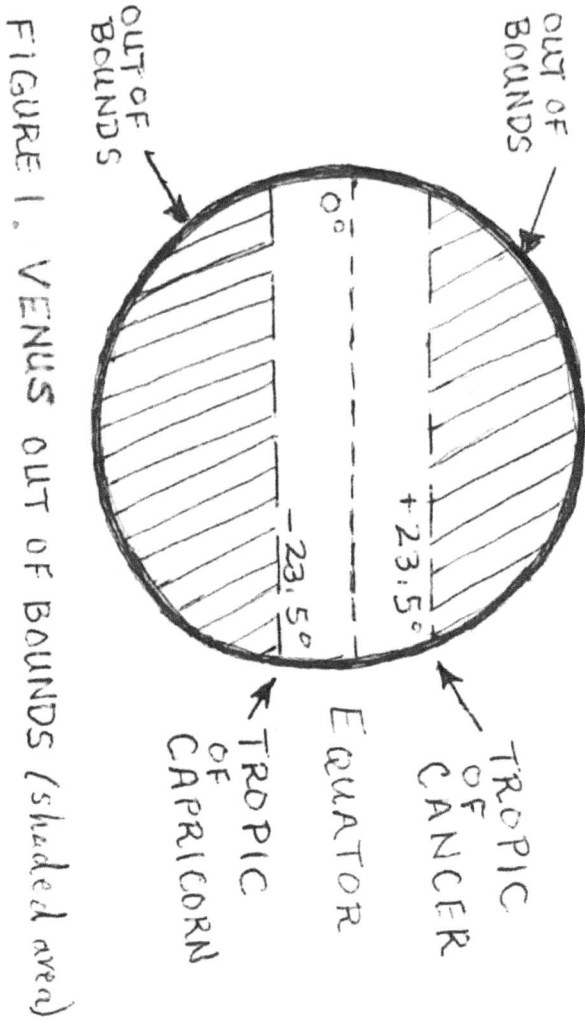

FIGURE 1. VENUS OUT OF BOUNDS (shaded area)

When a planet orbits this far outside of the Tropic of Cancer or Capricorn it is considered by astrologers to be acting Out of Bounds of its normal behavior. **The Out of Bound planet becomes more extreme in its behavior and is considered to have a very powerful influence on whatever it is in contact with.**

So for example, in a person's birth chart, if they have the planet Mars Out of Bounds they will have a very powerful effect when Mars is triggered astrologically. An analogy is living outside the comfort zone between the Tropic of Cancer and Capricorn. The further you live away from the equator and the closer you live to the poles the more powerful and extreme the weather and living conditions get.

An example in a presidential candidates chart; Trump has Mercury and Pluto Out of Bounds in his birth chart. Mercury is associated with communication and travel. He is the ultimate master at using communication, whether speaking, tweeting, or using the media to get his message across, and he is always on the go. He never seemed to wear out flying to multiple places day after day to give speeches during his Presidential campaign, in fact, this just seemed to energize him more. His tweets definitely can get voter and media attention. He also has Pluto Out of Bounds, which is associated with transformation and death, like tearing something down or transforming it in order to rebuild it into something new. Two of his major campaign promises were to repeal and replace Obama Care (the death of Obama Care) and the completion of the building of the Mexico border wall(transformation). G. W. Bush also has Pluto Out of Bounds, so expect similarities between these two Presidents in regards to things Pluto.

Let's return to applying the Venus Out of Bounds condition to the presidential election. We have established that Venus is always Out of Bounds every 8 years on Election Day due to the length of its synodic cycle and repeating pentagram pattern. **This means that the influence and power of Venus is extreme on Election Day and any candidate who has a strongly triggered Venus in their birth chart on that day will get a big boost.**

By taking the birth chart and progressing it to Election Day, an astrologer can see where Venus is active in their chart.

This tells the astrologer if the Election Day Venus Out of Bounds is empowered in their chart.

Let's review so far what has been established regarding Venus:

- the four year office of the President and election cycle is defined in the Constitution with the major designers such as George Washington, Benjamin Franklin, Thomas Jefferson, James Monroe, James Madison, Patrick Henry and many others who were Freemasons or closely associated with esoteric philosophy. The term of four years is likely based on sacred numerology.

- major events in the election cycle from the beginning of the primaries through the inauguration happen at predefined significant times in the astrological signs as shown in Table 2.

- the primaries end determining which of the major party candidates are chosen by getting the most primary votes determined in June during the sidereal sign of Taurus, a sign ruled by Venus

- the election occurs in early November, when the President elect is determined during the sidereal sign of Libra, a sign ruled by Venus

- every eight years the party that won has changed since 1952 as shown in Table 3

- the major 2 parties, Democrats and Republicans, have generally polar opposite political positions as shown in Table 4

- the 22nd Amendment to the Constitution to limit the Presidency to two terms of eight years, was advocated By Thomas F. Dewey, a prominent Freemason.

- Venus and Earth have a 1.6 year synodic cycle period that occurs exactly 5 times in an 8 year period. Venus returns to the same sign every 8 years in regards to its alignment to Earth during the election cycle in the sign of Libra, ruled by Venus

- The Venus- Earth synodic cycle is considered the most harmonic planetary energy system in the solar system in esoteric philosophy.

- Venus is Out of Bounds by latitude (declination) during the election in Libra every 8 years. An Out of Bounds Venus is considered powerful and extreme energy.

- An activated Venus in a candidates birth chart on Election Day will be empowered by the Out of Bounds Venus.

Chapter 4
The Trigger Man

In order to determine if the planet Venus is being triggered in a candidates chart on Election Day, the astrologer will progress the candidates chart to look at the declination cycle of Venus. However, in order for Venus to be triggered in that particular persons chart, another planet needs to come in contact with Venus. Trigger planets in astrology are the faster moving planets, such as the Moon, Mercury, or Mars. We will be using the Moon as the trigger planet in looking at the declination cycle of Venus. This can happen by triggering a candidate natal or progressed Venus. The natal (birth time) Venus is a fixed declination (never changes) and is shown as a straight line from the

time of birth in the declination chart. The progressed
Venus changes over time. Natal and progressed Venus
declinations are shown in Figure 2.

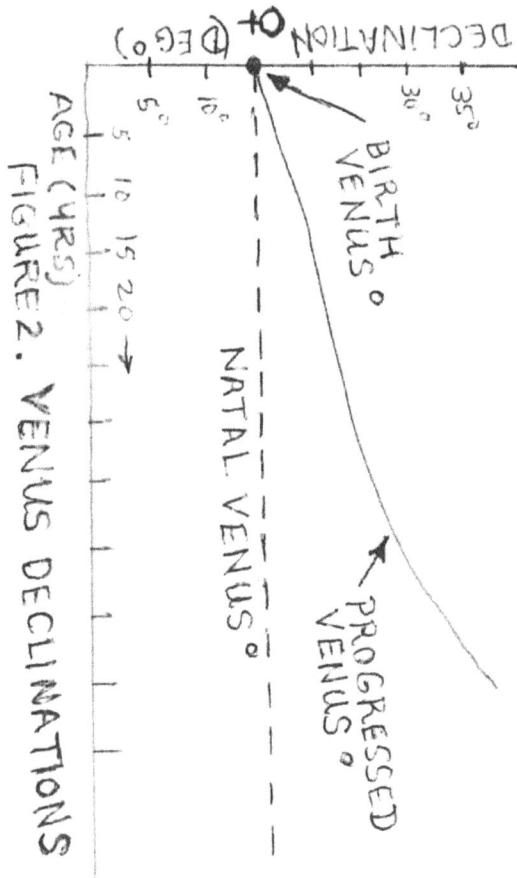

FIGURE 2. VENUS DECLINATIONS

The progressed Moon moves in the form of a sine
(repeating) wave. The Moon moves in this sine wave type

51

motion in a person's declination chart throughout their
lifetime. The peaks of the sine wave over time are called
wave peaks. The progressed Moon by declination and wave
peaks are shown in Figure 3.

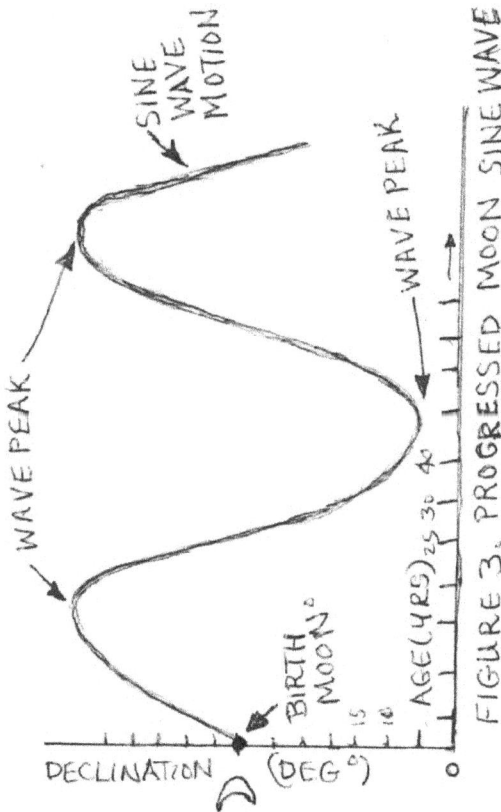

FIGURE 3. PROGRESSED MOON SINE WAVE

The progressed Moon triggers the effect of Venus in the chart at the specific time when it comes in contact with it. If this happens during an election year, it gives the candidate an advantage. The closer the timing of the contact between the Moon and Venus to the Election year; the more powerful the Venus influence is for that candidate. If it happens during a wave peak it tends to be a life climax and peak energy point such as in a career, marriage, income peak, etc. This trigger dynamic is shown in Figure 4.

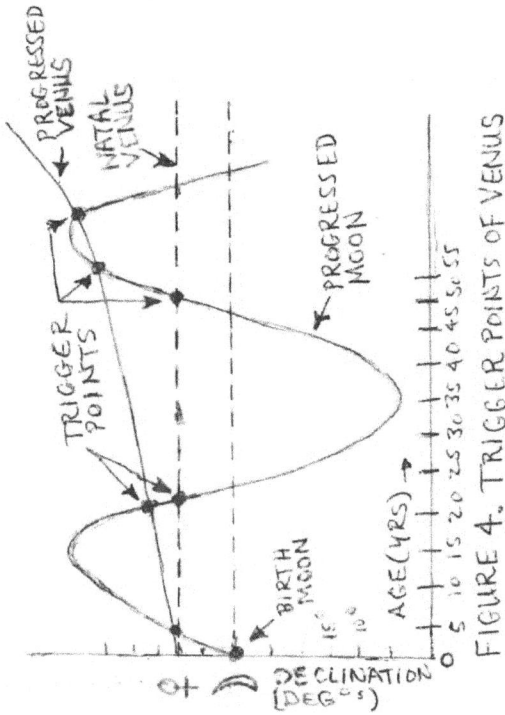

FIGURE 4. TRIGGER POINTS OF VENUS

Figure 4 only shows the intersection of the progressed
Moon with Venus over time for simplicity. In reality, the
declination chart will show all of the other planets
progressed and natal declinations. **Several planets can
contact the progressed Moon at the same time as Venus.
This indicates a concentration of the energies of the**

planets involved with Venus and is also important to look at as far as if they benefit Venus.

Approaching or applying energy is more powerful than separating energy. When the energy is occurring at the same time as the election Year, in astrology this is called conjunct, it is very powerful. It is similar to the Moon's monthly cycle when it is waxing or growing in size and power during its lunar cycle until it peaks at the full moon, and then it starts to decline or wane after the full moon passes until the end of its cycle. In this book, the trigger effect applying, conjunct, and separating in a range of five years is considered. Figure 5 shows how increments of half years (.5 years) are used to indicate the strength of a progressed Moon trigger of Venus in relation to the election year.

ELECTION
DAY

Applying   **Conjunct**   **Separating**

I   I   I   I   I   I   I   I   I   I
I
-2.5 -2.0 -1.5 -1.0 -.5   C   +.5 +1.0 +1.5 +2.0 +2.5 in years

Building Strong   Strongest   Strong   Weakening

Figure 5   Progressed Moon Trigger Strength

Let's look at the trigger effects of the Progressed Moon of
Venus for the presidential candidate McCain in the 2008
election race with Barack Obama.

Candidate	Election Year	Moon/Venus Trigger	Wave Peak	Other Planet Influences
McCain	2008	+2.0 (natal) weakening	no	Saturn

Table 6   Progressed Moon Triggers McCain 2008

The result is that in the election year 2008, McCain had a
separating, weakening progressed Moon and Venus contact
that did not occur in a wave peak. His Saturn had a small

influence on the progressed Moon trigger of Venus in the election year. Saturn can be either authoritative or restrictive. McCain lost the election to Barack Obama. We will determine why when we look at Barack Obama's progressed Moon in Chapter 5 and compare it with McCain's.

Chapter 5
Sweet Victory

Before we look at the winning Venus candidate signatures in the presidential elections, let's first examine the runner ups of the eight year Venus cycle election years starting with the Venus Out of Bounds election of 1952 and then the Venus Out of Bound elections every eight years through 2008 . This would be the candidates that won their party primary, but lost in the general election. We will look at the 2016 election in more detail as a separate case in detail since it is the most recent election in Chapter 6.

In Table 7 is the Venus trigger data for the eight races for the runner ups:

Candidate	Election Year	Venus Trigger	Wave Peak	Other Planet Influences
Stevenson	1952	-1.0 (natal) Strong	no	Mars
Nixon	1960	none	n/a	n/a
Humphrey	1968	+1.5 (natal) Strong -1.5 (natal) Strong	yes	Neptune
Ford	1976	none	n/a	n/a
Mondale	1984	none	n/a	n/a
G.H. Bush	1992	none	n/a	n/a
Gore	2000	none	n/a	n/a
McCain	2008	+2.0 (natal) Weakening	no	Saturn

Table 7   Venus Trigger Data – Runner Ups

Looking at the data of these eight runner ups, only three had any kind of Moon and Venus trigger going on at the time of the Election; Stevenson, Humphrey, and McCain. Stevenson and Humphrey both have strong Venus triggers, whereas McCain's is a weakening trigger. Of these three, only Humphrey has the trigger occurring during a wave peak. In the case of Stevenson and Humphrey who both have strong Venus triggers, why then were they not able to win the election? In order to answer this question we need to look at the winners and how they compare to the runner up in each general election of the Venus Out of Bounds elections between 1952- 2008. Comparing the data between the two general election candidates in a particular race will show the candidate with the stronger Venus attributes, and how that correlates with winning.

The next few pages will summarize each of the eight year Venus out of bounds election races. In the beginning of the book, it was mentioned that some people prefer to read tables with data organized in rows and columns and others prefer a summary in narrative form. I have generated both a data chart and narrative summary for each race.

For the charts, there are three types of information that are looked at in regards to Venus for each candidate:

- If the progressed Moon triggers either the natal (birth) or progressed Venus, its timing strength in the election year, (column titled "Moon/Venus Trigger")

- Whether the trigger occurs at a wave peak (column titled "Wave Peak")

- Other natal or progressed planet influences on Venus. This is noted only if the candidate Venus is already triggered by the progressed Moon (column titled "Other Planet Influences").

Bolded data indicates the Venus attributes that show a stronger position of the election winner in regards to the runner up.

For the narrative summary, the three types of information above are described in separate paragraphs, and then the winner rationale is summarized.

Year 1952	Candidate	Venus Trigger	Wave Peak	Other Planet Influences
Winner	Eisenhower	-1.0 prog **Strong** +2.0 natal Weakening	Yes	**Sun, Mars, Jupiter**
Loser	Stevenson	-1.0 natal Strong	No	Mars

Table 8   **1952 Election Day Race**

1952 Election Day Race
Eisenhower versus Stevenson

Venus Trigger:

Eisenhower has a strong progressed Moon trigger of Venus on Election Day.

Stevenson also has a strong progressed Moon trigger of Venus on Election Day.

Wave Peak (Life Peak):

Eisenhower's triggered Venus is occurring on a wave peak. This means his triggered Venus is happening during a very strong peak period of his life.

Stevenson's triggered Venus is not happening during a wave life peak so it is not as strong as Eisenhower's.

Other Planet Influences:

Eisenhower's triggered Venus is also supported by the Sun, Mars, and Jupiter which are either by birth or progression also occurring very close in time to the Election Day triggered Venus.

Stevenson is also supported by progressed Mars occurring very close in time to the Election Day triggered Venus.

Winner Rationale Summary:

Both Eisenhower and Stevenson have a progressed Moon triggered Venus, but Eisenhower's is happening during a very strong wave peak, and is supported by a greater amount of other planetary influences.

Eisenhower has the strongest Venus influences on Election Day and is the race winner.

Year 1960	Candidate	Venus Trigger	Wave Peak	Other Planet Influences
Winner	Kennedy	**-0.5 prog Strongest** -2.0 natal Building	**Yes**	**Sun, Mercury, Mars, Jupiter, Saturn, Neptune, Pluto**
Loser	Nixon	none	n/a	n/a

Table 9   1960 Election Day Race

1960 Election Day Race
Kennedy versus Nixon

Venus Trigger:

Kennedy has an extremely strong progressed Moon trigger of Venus on Election Day.

Nixon does not have a progressed Moon trigger of Venus on Election Day.

Wave Peak (Life Peak):

Kennedy's triggered Venus is occurring on a wave peak. This means his triggered Venus is happening during a very strong peak period of his life.

Nixon has no progressed Moon trigger of Venus, so this is not applicable.

Other Planet Influences:

Kennedy's triggered Venus is also supported by the influences of the Sun, Mercury, Mars, Jupiter, Saturn, Neptune, and Pluto which are either by birth or progression also occurring very close in time to the Election Day.

Nixon has no progressed Moon trigger of Venus, so this is not applicable.

Winner Rationale Summary:

Kennedy has an extremely strong progressed Moon trigger of Venus on Election Day, occurring during a wave peak, and is supported by seven other planetary influences on Election Day.

Nixon does not have a progressed Moon triggered Venus on Election Day.

Kennedy has the strongest Venus influences on Election Day and is the race winner.

Year 1968	Candidate	Venus Trigger	Wave Peak	Other Planet Influences
Winner	Nixon	C natal Strongest	No	Sun, Moon, Mars, Uranus
Loser	Humphrey	+1.5 natal Strong -1.5 natal Strong	Yes	Neptune

Table 10   1968 Election Day Race

1968 Election Day Race
Nixon versus Humphrey

Venus Trigger:

Nixon has an extremely strong progressed Moon trigger of Venus on Election Day.

Humphrey has a strong progressed Moon trigger of Venus on Election Day, but not as strong as Nixon's.

Wave Peak (Life Peak):

Nixon's triggered Venus is not occurring during a wave peak.

Humphrey's triggered Venus is occurring on a wave peak. This means his triggered Venus is happening during a peak period of his life.

Other Planet Influences:

Nixon's triggered Venus is also supported by the influences of the Sun, Moon, Mars, and Uranus which are either by birth or progression also occurring very close in time to the Election Day.

Humphrey's triggered Venus is supported by Neptune on Election Day.

Winner Rationale Summary:

Nixon has an extremely strong progressed Moon trigger of Venus on Election Day, which is supported by four other planetary influences on Election Day.

Humphrey has a progressed Moon trigger of Venus on Election Day but it is not as strong as Nixon's. Humphrey other planetary influence on Venus is Neptune on Election Day. Neptune tends to cause lack of clarity and focus and actually works against the progressed Moon trigger of Venus. Even though his Venus trigger is happening during a life peak this does not compensate for the stronger Nixon progressed Moon trigger of Nixon.

Nixon has the strongest Venus influences on Election Day and is the race winner.

Year 1976	Candidate	Venus Trigger	Wave Peak	Other Planet Influences
Winner	Carter	**-2.0 prog Building** +2.5 natal Weakening	No	**Mars, Saturn, Uranus**
Loser	Ford	None	n/a	n/a

Table 11   1976 Election Day Race

1976 Election Day Race
Carter versus Ford

Venus Trigger:

Carter has a weak progressed Moon trigger of Venus on Election Day.

Ford does not have a progressed Moon trigger of Venus on Election Day.

Wave Peak (Life Peak):

Carter's triggered Venus is not occurring during a wave peak.

Ford does not have a progressed Moon trigger of Venus on Election Day, so this is not applicable.

Other Planet Influences:

Carter's triggered Venus is also supported by a strong influence of Mars by progression occurring very close in time to the Election Day.

Ford does not have a progressed Moon trigger of Venus on Election Day, so this is not applicable.

Winner Rationale Summary:

Carter has a weak progressed Moon trigger of Venus on Election Day, which is supported by Mars, Saturn, and Uranus.

Ford does not have a progressed Moon trigger of Venus on Election Day.

Carter has the strongest Venus influences on Election Day and is the race winner.

Year 1984	Candidate	Venus Trigger	Wave Peak	Other Planet Influences
Winner	Reagan	-3.5 natal Building	No	Sun, Mercury, Mars, Jupiter,
Loser	Mondale	None	n/a	n/a

Table 12   1984 Election Day Race

1984 Election Day Race
Reagan versus Mondale

Venus Trigger:

Reagan has a very weak, but building progressed Moon trigger of Venus on Election Day.

Mondale does not have a progressed Moon trigger of Venus on Election Day.

Wave Peak (Life Peak):

Neither, Reagan or Mondale have a Venus trigger occurring on a wave peak on Election Day, so this is not applicable.

Other Planetary Influences:

Reagan's building Venus trigger is also supported by the Sun, Mars, Mercury, and Uranus (natal and progressed), and to a lesser extent by natal Jupiter.

Winner Rationale Summary:

Reagan has a weak but building progressed Moon trigger of Venus, and has several other planetary influences acting as a catalyst to support Venus on Election Day.

Mondale's Venus is completely out of cycle with Venus on Election Day, and therefore he does not have a progressed Moon trigger of Venus.

Reagan has the strongest Venus influences on Election Day and is the race winner.

Note: This election race was a reelection for Reagan. This may have changed the dynamics of Venus that were required to win. Possibly a Venus trigger does not have to be as strong to win in a reelection. This is the only case of a reelection during a Venus Out of Bounds election since 1952, so it is not possible to establish more than an outlier case for this.

In addition to the building Progressed Moon trigger of Venus, another additional Venus factor is at play for Reagan that will be covered in Chapter 7.

Year 1992	Candidate	Venus Trigger	Wave Peak	Other Planet Influences
Winner	B. Clinton	-1.0 prog Strong	Yes	n/a
Loser	G. H. Bush	None	n/a	n/a

Table 13   1992 Election Day Race

1992 Election Day Race
B. Clinton versus G.H. Bush

Venus Trigger:

B. Clinton has a strong progressed Moon trigger of Venus on Election Day.

G.H. Bush does not have a progressed Moon trigger of Venus on Election Day.

Wave Peak (Life Peak):

B. Clinton's triggered Venus is occurring on a wave peak. This means his triggered Venus is happening during a very strong peak period of his life.

G.H. Bush does not have a progressed Moon trigger of Venus on Election Day, so this is not applicable.

Other Planet Influences:

There are no other planetary influences involved for B. Clinton or G. H. Bush.

Winner Rationale Summary:

B. Clinton has a strong progressed Moon trigger of Venus on Election Day, which is also occurring during a wave (life) peak. G.H. Bush does not have a progressed Moon trigger of Venus on Election Day.

B. Clinton has the strongest Venus influences on Election Day and is the race winner.

Year 2000	Candidate	Venus Trigger	Wave Peak	Other Planet Influences
Winner	G. W. Bush	-2.0 prog Building +2.0 natal Weakening	No	Moon, Mars, Jupiter, Neptune
Loser	Gore	None	n/a	n/a

Table 14   2000 Election Day Race

2000 Election Day Race
G.W. Bush versus Gore

Venus Trigger:

G. W. Bush has a weak, but building progressed Moon trigger of Venus on Election Day.

Gore does not have a progressed Moon trigger of Venus on Election Day.

Wave Peak (Life Peak):

G.W. Bush's triggered Venus is not occurring on a wave peak.

Gore does not have a progressed Moon trigger of Venus on Election Day, so this is not applicable.

Other Planet Influences:

G.W. Bush's triggered Venus is also supported by the Moon, Mars, Jupiter, and Neptune which are either by birth or progression also occurring very close in time to the Election Day triggered Venus.

Gore does not have a progressed Moon trigger of Venus on Election Day, so this is not applicable.

Winner Rationale Summary:

G.W. Bush has a weak progressed Moon trigger of Venus on Election Day. G.W. Bush's triggered Venus is also supported by four planets which are either by birth or progression also occurring very close in time to the Election Day triggered Venus.

Gore does not have a progressed Moon trigger of Venus on Election Day.

G.W. Bush has the strongest Venus influences on Election Day and is the race winner.

Year 2008	Candidate	Venus Trigger	Wave Peak	Other Planet Influences
Winner	Obama	none	n/a	n/a
Loser	McCain	+2.0 natal Weakening	No	Mercury, Saturn

Table 15   2008 Election Day Race

2008 Election Day Race
Obama versus McCain

Venus Trigger:

Obama does not have a progressed Moon trigger of Venus on Election Day.

McCain has a weakening progressed Moon trigger of Venus on Election Day.

Wave Peak (Life Peak):

Neither Obama nor McCain have a progressed Moon trigger of Venus wave peak on Election Day

Other Planet Influences:

Obama does not have a progressed Moon trigger of Venus on Election Day so this is not applicable.

McCain's triggered Venus is also supported by Mercury and Saturn which are either by birth or progression also occurring very close in time to the Election Day.

Winner Rationale Summary:

Obama does not have a progressed Moon trigger of Venus
compared to the weak Progressed Moon trigger of McCain.
McCain also has the influence of two supporting planets.

McCain has the strongest Venus influences over Obama
and should have been the winner if looking at declinations
only. We will look at another factor related to Venus
besides using declinations that is a hidden weapon for
Obama compared to McCain in Chapter 7.

Chapter 6
2016

In the previous Chapter the eight Venus OOB election races between 1952 and 2008 were examined. They demonstrate a definite pattern for winning when comparing the winner to the runner up in each race. Let's now look at this pattern for winning in more detail.

The candidate with the strongest progressed Moon trigger of Venus wins. This is true regardless of whether it is occurring during a wave (life) peak or not. The wave peak serves to enhance the already present Venus trigger, but the strength of the Venus trigger trumps the wave peak. If the winner and loser have equally powerful Venus triggers, such as in the case of Eisenhower and Stevenson, the wave peak can intensify the trigger enough to produce a winner.

The other planets that are supporting also serve to enhance a strong Venus trigger, but do not trump it. They seem to really help outsiders and less politically experienced candidates win such as Kennedy and G.W. Bush who have a lot of supporting planets nearby to help Venus.

This is pretty amazing when you consider in the population as a whole, in many charts the progressed Moon never even transits Venus. In the case of these candidates, in order for Venus to be triggered, it has to be to be happening close to (within 2 to 3.5 years) of an eight year Venus OOB Election Day.

Let's now turn our attention to the 2016 election race. This was a race like no other. It was different from previous election races in the way the campaigns interacted with the electorate, the media and its ability to affect public opinion, skewing of polling and opinion surveys, interference from outside sources, campaign resignations, electorate influence, the number of candidates in the race (several were left almost up to the conventions) etc.

We will look at the race the same way we did for all the others, with both a chart and narrative summary. In addition to the winner and loser in the general election, we will also look at the some of the other candidates and potential candidates to see what their progressed Moon Venus triggers by declination looked like. With so many candidates in the race, what is it that makes only one prevail to win?

Year 2016	Candidate	Venus Trigger	Wave Peak	Other Planet Influences
Winner	Trump	C natal Strongest	Yes	Sun, Mercury, Saturn, Uranus, Pluto
Loser	H. Clinton	-2.5 natal Building	No	Sun, Moon, Mars, Neptune

Table 16   2016 Election Day Race

2016 Election Day Race
Trump versus H. Clinton

Venus Trigger:

Trump has an extremely strong progressed Moon trigger of Venus on Election Day.

H. Clinton has a building progressed Moon trigger of Venus on Election Day.

Wave Peak (Life Peak):

Trump's triggered Venus is occurring on a wave peak. This means his triggered Venus is happening during a peak period of his life.

H. Clinton's triggered Venus is not happening during a wave life peak.

Other Planet Influences:

Trump's triggered Venus is also strongly supported by the Sun, Mercury, Saturn, Uranus, and Pluto which are either by birth or progression also occurring very close in time to the Election Day triggered Venus.

H. Clinton's is also strongly supported by the Sun, Moon, Mars, and Neptune either by birth or progression also occurring very close in time to the Election Day triggered Venus.

Winner Rationale Summary:

Both Trump and H. Clinton have a progressed Moon triggered Venus, but Trump's is much stronger and is happening during a very strong life peak. His Venus is also supported by a greater amount and intensity of other planetary influences. Saturn, Uranus, and Pluto especially supported the theme of the authoritative (Saturn) outsider (Uranus), who energized the masses (Pluto) in this election.

Trump has the strongest Venus trigger on Election Day and is the race winner.

Trump has an extremely strong Venus activation on
Election Day 2016. The H. Clinton Venus is weak in
contrast and doesn't come close to competing with his. So
how did some of the other candidates or potential
candidates stack up, and who had the potential to beat him
in the race then?

First, let's look at some of the other candidates and
potential candidates on the Republican side. Since the
primary factor is whether or not they have a progressed
Moon trigger of Venus and how strong it is, we will only
look at that at this point.

Year 2016 Candidate	Venus Trigger		
Ryan (potential)	none		
Cruz	none		
Kasich	+1.5	prog	strong
J. Bush	none		
Rubio	-2.0	natal	building

Table 17   **Republican Potentials 2016**

Kasich and Rubio are the only candidates that had a progressed Moon trigger of Venus. Both Kasich and Rubio's are much weaker in comparison to that of Trump. Trump has the strongest Venus trigger.

It is interesting to note that Kasich has the second strongest Venus trigger and he stayed in the Republican primary the longest next to Trump.

Below is a list of candidates or potential candidates on the Democratic side besides H. Clinton.

Year 2016	Candidate	Venus Trigger		
	Sanders	none		
	Warren (potential)	+2.5	prog	weak
	Biden (potential)	C	natal	strongest

Table 18 – Democratic Potentials 2016

Sander's does not have a progressed Moon trigger of Venus. The potential candidate Warren has a weak progressed Moon trigger of Venus, which is not as strong as Trump's. However, the potential candidate Biden is a different story. He had a progressed Moon trigger of Venus just as strong as Trump's. His progressed Moon was conjunct his natal Venus, the strongest position possible, just like Trump's. Additionally, it is also occurring on a wave peak just like Trump's. He also had strong support from the Sun and Mercury. However, Trump has significantly more strongly supporting planets than Biden (Sun, Mercury, Saturn, Uranus, and Pluto). Using the Venus predictive method of this book, if anyone could have given Trump a more competitive race, it would have been Biden.

Biden never entered the race as a candidate, if he had, it would have been a very close race. We will never know if the extra supporting planets Trump had would have still been enough to carry him to victory, or if the political experience and recognition of Biden as a Senator and Vice President would have compensated for that more minor astrological factor. Biden would have had to shift the focus away from the planetary Trump helpers of Saturn, Uranus, and Pluto that defined the election theme of the authoritative, business (Saturn) outsider (Uranus), who energizes and supports the masses/populace (Pluto) in a way such that Trump could not have effectively activated those planetary energies available to him.

To summarize, a total of 9 presidential election races totaling 18 winners and runners up combined with 8 additional candidates or potential candidates in the 2016 race, for a total of 26 individuals or data points have been analyzed. Based on this data, the Venus astrological method using declinations shows for the winner:

- Progressed Moon trigger of Venus and its strength is the most important factor to produce a winner

- Wave peak is a common factor among winners, but does not trump the progressed Moon trigger of Venus strength; it is a supporting factor. If both the general election candidates have a progressed Moon trigger of Venus of the same strength, then the wave peak can act as a catalyst to propel one of the candidates to be the winner.

- other supporting planet influences close to the progressed Moon trigger of Venus are helpful and describe some of the winning characteristics or energies used, but are not the driver in determining a winner. Supporting planets are helpful to inexperienced political candidates.

Chapter 7
Venetian Blinds

There are two cases that need to be examined in more detail: the 1984 Reagan vs. Mondale and 2008 Obama vs. McCain races.

Reagan vs Mondale 1984: Mondale does not have a progressed Moon trigger of Venus. Reagan does have a weak, but building progressed Moon trigger of Venus of

-3.5 years

, which is further out in time than with the other winning presidential candidate races (the next closest winning candidate is -2.0 years).

Mondale has a losing declination chart; it is Reagan who does not seem to appear to have a very powerful winning declination chart.

Mondale's progressed Moon is completely out of phase, in other words, about as far away from Venus as you can get on Election Day; Reagan's is closer although very weak. Reagan's Venus trigger is technically stronger than Mondale's. However, there is another Venus factor that is helping Reagan.

Reagan has another Venus attribute at play that Mondale doesn't. Switching gears totally for a minute and looking at the two candidate's birth charts by longitude to Venus (not by declination), there is another Venus factor for Reagan using his 1911 birth chart. **He has a trine in his birth chart to the US birth chart Venus. It is important to note that the US birth chart Venus is also OOB.** In contrast, Mondale's birth chart does not have any major Venus aspects to the US birth chart Venus. This may have also helped Reagan win combined with his weak building progressed Moon trigger of Venus.

The natal trine of Venus would indicate a predestined relationship between Reagan and the US. The US birth chart is also activated on Election Day. Both the US birth chart and Election Day declination chart for 1984 have Venus Out of Bounds.

This election was unique in that this is the only election since 1952 that occurred on the eight year interval Venus Out of Bounds election that was a re-election for a sitting President. It is usually easier to become re-elected versus being elected for the first time. Maybe Reagan didn't need the push from Venus like in the other election races. Maybe the 3.5 year out progressed Moon trigger of Venus was enough. The birth chart Venus trine to the USA birth chart was there to further support him.

The other race we want to examine in more detail in this Chapter is the 2008 Obama vs. McCain race.

Obama's Venus is completely out of cycle with the progressed Moon much like Mondale's Venus in the 1984 race. McCain, even though he has a weak progressed Moon trigger to Venus, is still stronger than Obama's completely out of phase Progressed Moon to Venus. **One secret weapon Obama does have going for him, just like Reagan in the 1984 race, is a strong aspect in his birth chart to Venus. His birth chart Venus conjuncts the US birth chart Out of Bounds Venus. This is a very strong aspect to Venus and indicates a predestined relationship between Obama and the US.**

This leads us to another presidential election Venus factor to consider in determining a winner. A strong birth chart aspect of Venus to the US birth chart Venus (which is Out of Bounds), can work in the same way as having a progressed Moon trigger of Venus Out Of Bounds by declination near the time of the Election Day.

Chapter 8
Illusions of Choice

Astrology is the "astro" (space) "logy" (knowledge) of the galaxy, including this planet we call Earth and the beings we call humans. Coming full circle back to the opening comments of this book, astrology is not just something humans thought of over time from observed patterns, or divined using magic from demons, it was taught to humans on Earth by the Watcher Baraqiel (also spelled Baraqijal, or Baraqel). Other terms also used for the Watchers are God(s), Extraterrestrials, Space Travelers. The Watchers, according to the Book of Enoch, came to Earth to seed this planet (Humanity being part of that) a long time ago, and who taught humans astrology based on their advanced understanding of science and space. Humans were taught astrology by the time of the prophet Enoch in the region of the early developing civilization of Babylon (today the Middle East area of Iraq). This is documented in the Book of Enoch, a historically recognized ancient religious document (see Appendix II). The Watchers knew the influences of the galaxies, constellations, solar systems, black holes, planets, and other celestial forces based on scientific principals such as frequency, wavelength, principals of motion, cause and effect, harmonics, etc. This is what astrology is based on and why it works.

In this book a logical approach to astrology has been used based on data using an objective approach of trends, patterns, and data analysis throughout history.

This book has concentrated only on the function of Venus as it relates to US presidential elections. Why Venus? Venus has had a hidden hand in virtually every facet of the US presidential election process from the beginning of the nation. Let's review all of the factors associated with Venus we have explored in this book:

 - The four year election cycle is defined in Article II of the Constitution with the major designers such as George

Washington, Benjamin Franklin, Thomas Jefferson, James Monroe, James Madison, Patrick Henry and many others who were Free Masons or closely associated with esoteric principles. The term of four years is likely based on ancient numerology, and denotes a perfect term for the appointed ruler by God.

- Major events in the election cycle from the beginning of the primaries through the inauguration happen at predefined significant times in the astrological signs

- The primaries end determining which of the major party candidates are chosen by getting the most primary votes determined in June during the sidereal sign of Taurus, a sign ruled by Venus

- The election occurs in early November, when the President elect is determined during the sidereal sign of Libra, a sign ruled by Venus

- Every 8 years the party that won has changed since 1952 between the major 2 parties. Democrats and Republicans have generally polar opposite political positions.

- The 22nd Amendment to the Constitution to limit the Presidency to two terms of 8 years, was advocated By Thomas F. Dewey, a prominent Free Mason.

- Venus and Earth have an 8 year synodic cycle. This means Venus returns to the same place every 8 years in regards to its alignment to Earth during the election cycle.

- Venus and Earth have a 1.6 year synodic cycle period that occurs exactly 5 times in the 8 year period. Venus returns to the same place every 8 years in regards to its alignment to Earth during the election cycle in the sign of Libra, a sign ruled by Venus.

- The Venus- Earth synodic cycle is considered the most harmonic planetary energy system in the solar system.

- Venus is Out of Bounds by latitude (declination) during the election in Libra every 8 years. An Out of Bounds Venus is considered powerful and extreme energy in Astrology.

- The progressed Moon triggers the effect of Venus in the chart at the specific time when it comes in close contact with it. If this happens during an election year, it gives the candidate an advantage. The closer the timing of the aspect between the Moon and Venus to the Election year; the more powerful the Venus influence is for that candidate.

The Moon moves like a sine wave motion in a person's declination chart throughout their lifetime. Transits to the progressed Moon during a wave peak tend to be life path climax points, such as a career high, marriage, or financial success.

- Progressed Moon trigger of Venus and its strength is the most important factor to produce a winner

- Wave peak is a common factor among winners, but does not trump the progressed Moon trigger of Venus strength, it is a supporting factor. If both the general election candidates have a progressed Moon trigger of Venus of about the same strength, then the wave peak can act as a catalyst to propel one of the candidates to be the winner.

- other supporting planetary influences close to the progressed Moon trigger of Venus are helpful and describe some of the winning characteristics or energies used, but are not the driver in determining a winner. Supporting planets are especially helpful to inexperienced political candidates.

- If neither general election candidate has a progressed Moon trigger of the Election Day Out of Bounds Venus or a very weak one, then a candidate can also win by having a major supporting aspect, such as a trine or conjunction, of

their birth chart Venus to the US birth chart Out of Bounds
Venus.

Applying these principles and rules result in the prediction
of the winning presidential candidate in all 9 races
examined. It also explains results for the runner ups, and
some of the other candidates and potential candidates that
dropped out during the race. This data is sufficient to show
a definite pattern or trend based on astrological aspects of
Venus. There is just too much supporting data here to
consider this as coincidence or random outcomes.

As more Venus Out of Bounds elections occur and more
data is able to be collected, the better the understanding of
the influence of Venus and the confidence level of the
outcomes will be increased. Adjustments may need to be
made to the Venus theory presented here over time and as
more data becomes available, just as is done with scientific
theories.

Astrology works much like science. In fact, throughout
most of history, astrology and astronomy were

interconnected. It was common for an astrologer to also be a mathematician, physicist, chemist, etc. Many of the leading, progressive scientists were also astrologers, such as Keplar and Newton. It wasn't until the 1700's that a separation occurred, which is now slowly being reversed.

Scientific principles are present within astrology. For example, look at the principal of potential vs kinetic energy. The natal or birth chart of any person is fixed in time and space. It is unique to the person, just like a fingerprint. Even twins are born at least seconds apart and in slightly different physical points in space. The birth chart is the potential astrological energy map of that person. Once the birth time and place are fixed, all astrological influences, such as transits, aspects, and declinations throughout time are fixed as part of the individual earthly sojourn. Some people choose to utilize or fulfill more of their potential energy than others.

Just because you were born with the potential to become president of the US, doesn't mean you will become one. That's because humans are also born with free will. They must apply their free will and then turn that into action in order to convert their potential energy into kinetic energy.

To maximize the effectiveness of their actions, timing is also critical. Just like our winning presidential candidates, they put all of their energy into building their campaigns, running their races, and at a time when they could be most effective. "Timing is Every Thing" is a common phrase to represent this. If they had tried to do the same thing, and worked just as hard 10 years later, it wouldn't have worked for them in the same way or not at all. It's like the example of a trend that is really popular for a year. Trying to repeat it again in a few years doesn't work because that window in time is gone for that specific type of potential energy to be present and converted to kinetic energy.

Another principle of physics applies here, it takes a lot more energy to travel upstream than downstream. "Go with the Flow" is a common metaphysical principle that is also demonstrated by science. This is one of the biggest advantages in knowing your astrology chart and then looking at a point in time, which is called a transit. You can see what energy is active and available at that point in time; then maximize its use.

For example, I was debating about selling my house in the fall of 2013. I was planning on moving sometime in the next year but wasn't sure how productive trying to sell my house in the fall would be. In the geographic area I lived in, late spring (May/June) was the most popular time for families to buy houses and get settled in before school started in August, thus creating the most demand and higher prices paid for houses. I had missed the spring and summer to get the house flipped and on the market. I looked at my astrology chart and transits for the fall. My Saturn was going to transit the 12th house. In a couple of more years I would also have a Saturn return. Saturn rules real estate and one of the things the 12th house represents is endings. The time leading up to a Saturn return is typically not a good time to make significant new life changes or take on new large projects with long lasting effects. However, it is a good time for closure to make way for the new that will be occurring during the Saturn return. So looking at my chart indicated, in my case, that fall was a good time to sell my house. Closure of that chapter of my life, which flipping and selling my house was a part of, to prepare for the new coming up in a couple of years was favored; the timing was right. I flipped and sold the house in November successfully and even had to hustle to get all my stuff out by the end of November when the buyers wanted to move in. This worked for me because the potential energy to sell my house was available to me at that time. I was in the flow of my astrology chart.

Clients have asked me "What if I choose to work against my chart?" My answer is "You can, you have free will, but it is more difficult and likely will not result in the best outcome for you. " So let's go back to my chart when I sold my house successfully and quickly. If instead I would have stayed in the house and tried to start a business at that time, things would have turned out very different. That time was not the time to start new ventures for me, like starting a business. It would have been too soon, and the resources and support would not have been there to be successful. I would not have been ready and would have struggled. Waiting to sell the house until the next spring would have been outside the optimal window astrologically for doing that. I likely would have lost money in the end in comparison to selling it the previous fall, and created a lot more work and struggle for myself.

Why choose to work against your chart? Knowing your birth chart and how to work with its energies and timing is the beauty of astrology. You can then focus your energy on areas that have the potential to yield the most successful outcomes at a given time.

Another way to look at the birth chart potential energy is as destiny or providence. Some people have felt destined their whole life to be and do certain things. I think some people are more able to empathically feel their chart without cognitively being aware of it. What you do with potential becomes action, motion, or kinetic energy.

Isn't this really what they teach you in self- help seminars? Reach within yourself, know yourself, reflect on what is not working, and then establish what your desired goal is in life. Develop a plan to achieve and reinforce this within yourself. Then act on it with focused intention.

The big difference with astrology is you can know and confirm your potential through your birth chart on a more cognitive level and tap into its timing mechanism to assist you in doing things at the most auspicious time for maximum results.

Astrology is a very powerful tool. That's why throughout history Rulers, Orders, Secret Societies, Court Seers/Advisors, Kabbalists, Magi in the Bible, etc. who served the elite of humanity have used astrology to make decisions on virtually everything. They don't want the general public to know about it because then they could use it and in the end that would lessen the power they have over them. So it's given an image that it has no basis in logic or a demonic image to scare people away. Many world leader, famous, and wealthy people use it.

The global elite of today still know and use astrology. Astrology has been used (mostly by the elite) on the Earth since humans have been on the Earth. Important dates, speeches, investments, events, and cycles are set according to astrology. Why do you think Christmas is on December 25th when historically Jesus birth date is considered to be in the spring? Because December 25th occurs in the sign of Sagittarius, whose natural ruler is Jupiter in the 9th house. The 9th house rules religion. Jupiter is also the most expansive and beneficial planet there is, and that's why it rules wealth. If you're a retailer, you want Christmas in the sign of Sagittarius- the best energetic period of the year to produce wealth based on a religious theme!

Why is Labor Day celebrated on the first Monday in September? Because this is in the sign of Leo whose natural ruler is the Sun in the 5th house. The Sun is the energy center for our solar system, its life blood. The 5th house is the house of creativity, self-expression, and potential. If the elite are going to show off their work force to the rest of the world, they want it at its energetic best.

Why is Thanksgiving on the fourth Thursday of November? Because it is in the sign of Scorpio whose natural rulers are Mars and Pluto in the 8th house. Mars is ruled by Aries the most intense fire sign in the zodiac and is a planet of action, industry, and courage. Pluto is a sign of the people as a collective and power. The eighth house is about shared resources and inheritance. Even the ancient symbol for Scorpio was the Phoenix; a big bird, and what is the central feast centerpiece on the Thanksgiving dinner table, and what do we do with that big bird on Thanksgiving? We become one with it, so to speak! You can go through every major holiday throughout the year and correlate it to its astrological sign in this way.

Note: Recall the use the ancient sidereal sun signs, not the tropical sun sign system (reference Appendix I).

Returning to politics, in a political campaign a candidate has to align their energy with the energy of the voters. For example, in 2016 voters were looking for a non-status quo candidate and found it in Trump. What is really tricky is what sets the intention of the voters? **Or more specifically, what sets the intention of the majority of voters needed to elect a president**?

We saw in Chapter 2 that the party of the elected president has changed every eight years when there is a Venus Out of Bounds election since 1952. The two party System represents polar opposite positions on governance. Elections oscillate back and forth between parties and ideologies much like the function of the progressed Moon

sinusoidal wave motion that triggers Venus in the
declination chart within the repeating harmonic planetary
energy of the Venus– Earth eight year synodic cycle.

In fact the definition of a harmonic is that it is a repeating
signal, such as a sinusoidal wave.

Johannes Keplar, a 16th century German mathematician,
astronomer, and astrologer, in his work "Harmonices
Mundi" ("The Harmony of the World" written in 1619),
explains his discovery of the Third Law of Planetary
Motion. His theory is based on the concept that harmonics
applies to the alignment of heavenly bodies.

"While medieval philosophers, spoke metaphysically of the
"Music of the Spheres"; Keplar discovered physical
harmonies in planetary motion. He found that the
difference between maximum and minimum angular speeds
of a planet in its orbit approximates a harmonic
proportion." [9]

Keplar claimed that the principle of harmonics applied to
nature, as well as to celestial and terrestrial bodies that

interact with the human soul as well as the Earth soul. Kepler defined an astrological harmonic system of the planets. It involves complex mathematics, geometry, and physics which is beyond the scope of this book to explain. The main concept take away we want to work with is that he defined harmonics between the planets; one of them being between Venus and the Earth.

The theory of how the techniques in this book work integrates with what Kepler defined centuries ago in his Third Law of Planetary Motion.

Combining the harmonic energy of Venus and Earth as they are acted upon (triggered) by the Moon, creates the repeating harmonic cycle every 8 years triggered by the sinusoidal wave motion of the Moon. **The Venus, Earth, and Moon act together as a timing mechanism for the expression of the Earth consciousness or soul over time.** This energy works at a planetary level, and appears more subtle than the transits working in a particular persons birth chart.

We are more in tune to our individual birth chart energies, but not as aware of the cosmic forces also at play in our lives all the time on a more group or planetary level. This subtle energy is the type of energy that acts at the group level, which produces the energy pattern or harmonic of the majority consensus of voters in an election. Some people are aware of it to a degree on the group level, but do not realize it is acting on their individual soul level as well. An analogy is like how the grains of sand act to form a beach. All of the grains of sand are influenced on an individual consciousness level to form the essence of sand as well as at a group level to form the beach. So to humans have their individual birth chart destiny to act out as well as their role to play as part of the group consciousness of Earth.

These subtle harmonic energies of Venus are activated during the presidential race. If the candidate also has Venus triggered by the progressed Moon or a Natal Venus aspect to the US Venus on Election Day, then they are "in the flow" of the Venus-Earth synodic cycle energy, and are therefore favored.

The integration of astrology with science is in its infancy in the author's opinion. We have only just begun to understand the subtle forces at work in our galaxy; the constellations, black holes, solar and lunar energies, etc. that affect us as humans on this planet. Likewise, refinement of this theory as more data and scientific understanding becomes available that further integrates the physics and metaphysics of the astrological effects of Venus may be needed. The key to the Venus theory usefulness is: Does it work in predicting the election winner at a high level of reliability over time?

The next Venus Out of Bounds election is in 2024. It seems like a long time away, but it is possible to run the chart for this Election Day and of potential candidates at any time. Of course, the closer the election, the more decided the actual candidates and resolution of the data to work with will be. If the presidential campaigns read this book and apply the techniques, will this make the race more competitive? Can pre knowledge of the effects of Venus detailed in this book effect the race and results?

The chosen candidate needs to:

- have the potential energy (destiny) to be president in their birth chart by having a Venus that can yield a winner during one of the eight year election cycles of Venus Out of Bounds (the next one is 2024)

- use their free will to act on their birth chart potential (enter the race and apply themselves fully)

- be in the right race at the right time according to their progressed Moon trigger of Venus by declination (the right timing for running)

- have a stronger progressed Moon trigger of Venus than the other candidates in their primary as well as the general election, OR a birth chart Venus aspect strong enough to counter an opponents progressed Moon trigger of Venus (be the strongest overall candidate in the field based on the techniques of this book)

If the Elite have known and applied the influence of the plant Venus Out of Bounds all along, then the Elite already know the outcome of an election before the vote. Although in the 2016 election, the elite didn't seem to get it right in both the primaries and general election. They were shocked at the end result of the election. Either that or they want people to believe the election result was an upset, but in reality that was the plan.

On the other hand, if the Elite were not aware and used a significantly different astrological method other than that described in this book, they may incorporate the use of this method in the future.

One of the first things to look for in 2024 is the Venus trigger profiles of the most likely candidates. Who has a progressed Moon trigger of Venus and which is the strongest candidate. A level of sophistication that could be applied is to purposely create a field of party candidates, knowing which one of the candidates has the strongest Venus trigger, that being of course the candidate desired to win the party nomination in the end.

One take away in all of this is that we live in a complex Universe of interacting energies that work together at levels that individuals are mostly unaware of, nor of their energetic influences on us. The Universe is ordered, just like the birth chart of an individual is ordered from the moment of birth. Both are part of the force called creation. Our lives, our choices are not just random events and outcomes occurring, we are part of a much larger energy at work that operates on various planes of existence simultaneously; galactic, constellational, planetary, country, group, and individual. It is all part of the whole of creation. In physics, this is called entanglement theory. Science is learning that all things are interconnected.

The Venus influences on the presidential election shows that the planetary energies of Venus affect the US voters as a group soul and we receive that cosmic energy and integrate that into our being on the individual soul level. As Keplar postulated; humans resonate with the energies and harmonics within the Universe and fulfill their purpose as part of that energy wave or life force. Most of the time, we are not even consciously aware of it. It is happening on a subconscious level just like the majority of our bodily functions which are controlled by the autonomic centers in our body. There is no way we could maintain our bodily needs with our minds, it would overwhelm our mental ability to function.

We are all part of a larger plan and logic of the Universe. Humans on Earth are as much a part of the cosmic stream as anything else in the universe. It is about being in harmony with the cosmic flow, or what is called the State of Being. **Yes, we have free will and individual choice, either to be in harmony with the cosmic flow or not. It is easier to be in the flow, taking the path of least resistance. Therefore, ……..and this is key…….., most will choose to be in the flow creating the group consciousness which then prevails and propels Universal evolution forward.**

This is what the Watcher Baraqel (also spelled Baraqijal, Baraqiel) taught humans as a universal creational system of interconnected time, space, energy, frequencies, harmonics, logic, and evolution that is called astrology today.

References

1   https://en.wikipedia.org/wiki/Book of Enoch

2   https://en.wikipedia.org/wiki/Book of Enoch #The   Book of the Watchers

3   https:// en.wikipedia.org/wiki/Constitution of the United States of America

4   https://en.wikipedia.org/wiki/Tetragrammation

5   https:// en.wikipedia.org/wiki/List of Presidents of the United States who were Freemasons

6   https:// en.wikipedia.org/wiki/Twenty Second Amendment to the United States Constitution

7   "Morals and Dogma of the Ancient and Accepted Scottish Rite of Freemasonry, prepared for the Supreme Council of the Thirty Third Degree for the Southern Jurisdiction of the United States", by Albert Pike, Charleston, 1871, first published 1872

8   https://en.wikipedia.org/wiki/orbital period

9   https://en.wikipedia.org/wiki/Harmonices Mundi

List of Figures

List of Tables

Appendix I

SIDEREAL ZODIAC SIGNS

SUN SIGN	SIDEREAL DATE RANGE
Aries	15 April-15 May
Taurus	16 May- 15 June
Gemini	16 June-15 July
Cancer	16 July-15 August
Leo	16 August-15 September
Virgo	16 September-15 October
Libra	16 October- 16 November
Scorpio	16 November- 15 December
Sagittarius	16 December-14 January
Capricorn	15 January- 14 February
Aquarius	15 February- 14 March
Pisces	15 March-14 April

Appendix II

The Book of Enoch

Excerpt

The Book of the Watchers (1 Enoch 1–36)

Source:
https://en.wikipedia.org/wiki/Book_of_Enoch#The_Book_of_the_Watchers

And Azâzêl taught men to make swords, and knives, and shields, and breastplates, and made known to them the metals of the earth and the art of working them, and bracelets, and ornaments, and the use of antimony, and the beautifying of the eyelids, and all kinds of costly stones, and all colouring tinctures. And there arose much godlessness, and they committed fornication, and they were led astray, and became corrupt in all their ways. Semjâzâ taught enchantments, and root-cuttings, Armârôs the resolving of enchantments, **Barâqîjâl, taught astrology**, Kôkabêl the constellations, Ezêqêêl the knowledge of the clouds, Araqiêl the signs of the earth, Shamsiêl the signs of the sun, and Sariêl the course of the moon.

Appendix III

Pentagram of Venus

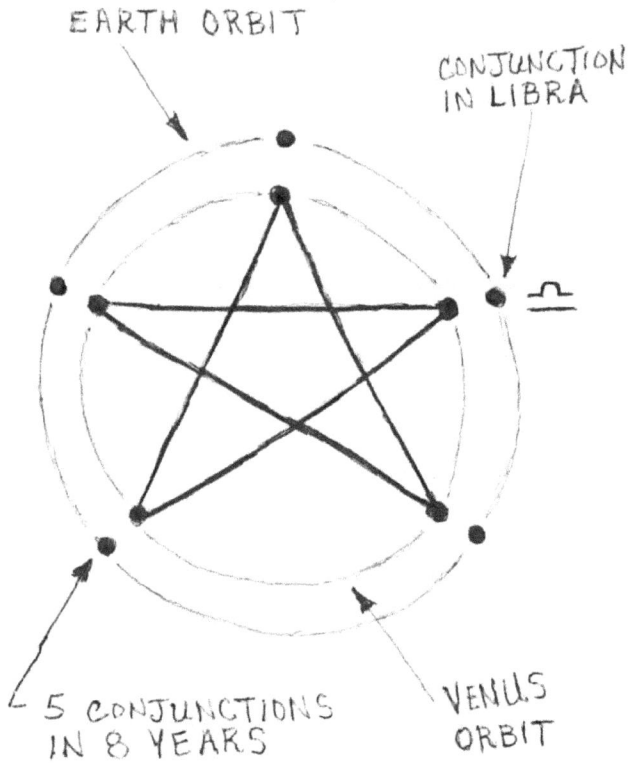

EARTH ORBIT

CONJUNCTION IN LIBRA

5 CONJUNCTIONS IN 8 YEARS

VENUS ORBIT

Venus moves in a pentagram motion in relationship to the Earth. It repeats 5 inferior conjunctions every 8 years. One of these conjunctions occurs in the sign of Libra during the US presidential election.

EPIC TRUTH ASTROLOGICAL SERVICES

Discover your unique astrological story! Your astrological birth chart reveals your potential and soul purpose in this lifetime on Earth.

Birth Chart Drivers and Soul Purpose Report

Your chart drivers are the major astrological aspects in your birth chart having the largest impact on your life. They are the most powerful tools in your astrological tool kit. Learn what they are and how to use them to their maximum potential. The lunar nodes describe your past life journey and Soul purpose in this lifetime. Your south node describes the soul experiences from the past life you are coming from. The north node is your soul personality, the composite of all your past lives, and its continuing purpose in this life. Saturn sets the timing of the evolutionary cycles set into motion in your birth chart. Each cycle has a major function or theme and junction points where changes can most effectively be implemented. Pluto is the planet of transformation and power. It describes the transformational focus in this lifetime and sources of power that you have developed over many lifetimes available to you to achieve your evolutionary intent.

This is a custom report prepared just for you.

To order Epic Truth astrological reports and services go to:

www.forepictruth.com **or email us at** forepictruth@gmail.com

www.ingramcontent.com/pod-product-compliance
Lightning Source LLC
Chambersburg PA
CBHW060940040426

42445CB00011B/940